The Plain People:

A Glimpse at Life Among
the Old Order Mennonites of Ontario

The Plain People:

A Glimpse at Life Among
the Old Order Mennonites of Ontario

John F. Peters

Photographs by Carl Hiebert

Published by Pandora Press
Co-published with
Herald Press
2003

National Library of Canada Cataloguing in Publication

Peters, John F. (John Fred), 1935-
    The plain people: a glimpse at life among the Old Order Mennonites of Ontario /
John F. Peters; Carl Hiebert, photographer.

Includes bibliographical references.
ISBN 1-894710-26-6

    1. Old Order Mennonites—Ontario—Social conditions. I. Hiebert, Carl, 1947-
II. Title.

BX8129.O43P48 2002   305.6'870713   C2003-900035-4

The Plain People: A Glimpse at Life Among the Old Order Mennonites of Ontario
    Copyright©2003 by Pandora Press
    33 Kent Avenue
    Kitchener, Ontario N2G 3R2
    www.pandorapress.com
    All rights reserved.

Co-published with Herald Press
Scottdale, Pennsylvania/Waterloo, Ontario

International Standard Book Number: 1-894710-26-6

Cover design by Clifford Snyder
Book design by Julia Stark.

13 12 11 10 09 08 07 06 05 04 03   12 11 10 9 8 7 6 5 4 3 2 1

*This book is dedicated to all who seek
to follow Jesus in simplicity, quietness, and peacefulness—
qualities found among the old orders.*

Table of Contents

Acknowledgements

Recognizing those who have contributed to the writing of a book is a daunting task. Someone will be omitted! And too, where should I begin–with both my grandmothers? They, along with parents, teachers, school friends, and possibly even my childhood dog, Bowser, undoubtedly made some contribution. I gladly follow tradition here.

My wife, Lorraine, always lent a listening ear and support in my ecstasy about another "discovery" after each visit to the old orders. A few times she accompanied me, and together we enjoyed old order food graciously provided by our hosts. Lorraine gave practical advice to sensitive issues and was patient through the writing process.

I owe a special thanks to many old order friends and acquaintances who assisted me in my search, many knowingly, some unwittingly. Most treated me with suspicion upon first contact, and with time showed kindness and tolerance. I appreciate these many contacts in various settings: barns (often in the cold), farmyards, shops, homes, church, and a few times in travel and in our home. I have learned much, and greatly respect their way of life. I am deeply indebted to two old orders who have read an early draft of this manuscript. I omit their names out of sensitivity to their way of life; that is, not being prominent, and living in a humble manner.

I have also spoken with a few who have left the community, and others outside the old order community. This has expanded my understanding. Dennis Lehto has given his time and technical skills in scanning the photographic work. Abe Thiessen, Miriam Frey and Ruby Schmidt have all very carefully read the entire manuscript and offered constructive comments. Their insights have done much to lift the fog, accumulated through the many revisions made by the author. I take full responsibility for the final writing which is now in your hands.

It has been a great pleasure working with Pandora Press. They joined me in the enthusiasm of producing this book, and their appreciation of Mennonite history and life was a rich asset. Julia Stark applied her skills, transforming computer screens full of words and matrices of pixels to a visual delight.

I am deeply indebted to a recognized Canadian photographer and friend, Carl Hiebert. He has been on this journey of making life meaningful, and impacting people to "make a difference." He has graciously provided all the pictures in this book. Every reader will quickly recognize the contribution this has made in telling the story.

John F. Peters

Preface

My first introduction to the Old Order Mennonites was made in a university classroom. In 1970 I was new to the Waterloo area. A Mennonite professor had invited a minister with a black suit and no tie, and a grade eight education, to speak to students who had spent almost twice the time in school classrooms as the guest speaker. Ten years later I reestablished contact with this man and his wife, on their farm, and a friendship developed. This contact led to numerous other associations with the Old Order Mennonites, at times referred to as the "plain and simple" or "peculiar and separate" people.

As a sociologist, intrigue led to a search to better understand the pulse of the Old Order Mennonites. Many people form impressions from seeing these folk dressed in black or navy blue, at the market, or from passing them on the street, either walking or travelling by horse and buggy. This book is an attempt to bring a better understanding and appreciation to another stripe in the mosaic of Canadian cultures.

John F. Peters

Mennonites

We Begin

There are more than a million Mennonites residing in almost every country of the world. The vast majority mix well into their surrounding culture, and are not distinct in their work, dress, recreation, or place and style of residence. They would not be considered "separate and peculiar." In ideal terms, Mennonites aspire to be peace-oriented, become involved in the needs of people locally or abroad (either through the church or through such agencies as Mennonite Central Committee), and endeavour to practice the teachings of Christ as found particularly in the "sermon on the mount" (Matthew 5-7).

Mennonite belief arose out of the Reformation. The break from the state church happened in 1525, principally over the practice of adult baptism. Those who followed this practice immediately experienced imprisonment, fines and torture. This Anabaptist belief spread to Germany and the Netherlands. By 1536 a Roman Catholic priest by the name of Menno Simons, dissatisfied with church and political activity, studied the Bible, and went public with his theology. Followers were eventually named Mennonites. They continued to endure severe suffering, even death, for their faith. Old Order Mennonites place this suffering of their forefathers very central in their theology. Many of the Dutch group emigrated to what is now Poland, then in the latter half of the seventeenth century to Russia. They are sometimes identified as "Russian" Mennonites, some of whom emigrated to the United States and Canada in three waves: 1873-1884, 1922-1930, (with some going to Paraguay, Brazil and Mexico), and soon after WW II.[1]

---

[1] The author's wife's paternal grandfather came to Canada in the first wave. His mother's parents came to Canada in 1905, and his father in 1925.

The majority of the Swiss Mennonites emigrated in the eighteenth century, and were welcomed to the Pennsylvania area by William Penn, a Quaker. In the fifty-year period after 1785 about two thousand Swiss Mennonites emigrated from the United States to Canada by Conestoga buggy over the Niagara river. They pioneered the virgin soil of the land.

During those pioneer days, Swiss Mennonites lived very much like their neighbours. However, with industrialization and a more evangelical and individualistic understanding of one's relationship with God between 1872 and 1913, the uniqueness of the old order developed. In the mid 1800s some became more secular, others more pietistic. In 1889 a major division occurred, with the majority forming a more liberal group, known as Old Mennonite. They have since changed their name several times and have numerous churches in Kitchener-Waterloo and surrounding area. A more detailed explanation of Mennonite origins, as well as their presence in modern life, can be found in Appendix I.

Old order Mennonites make up approximately ten per cent of the Canadian and American Mennonite population. They represent possibly more than twenty per cent of all Mennonites in Ontario and speak the Pennsylvania Dietch (not Dutch) dialect. Amish are correctly considered old orders. They separated from the Mennonites in Europe in 1693. There are close to three thousand Amish in Ontario, living in the Aylmer and Wellesley areas, west of the old order Mennonites. They have no meeting houses (churches). They do not use electricity, and men grow beards. More detail on the Amish is available in Appendix II.

Old Orders
Tradition with Order

All old order Canadian Mennonites are located in Southern Ontario. In the fifties and sixties almost all lived in the region immediately north, northwest, and northeast of the city of Waterloo. At that time all children attended small local public schools, to which they could either walk, or be driven by a parent in horse and buggy. They then spread to four other areas: north of Mount Forest (120 km. north of Waterloo), near Pembroke (200 km. northwest of Ottawa), near Lucknow, (about 190 km. northwest of Waterloo), and Chesley, (60 km. northwest of Mount Forest) (See Map 1). More

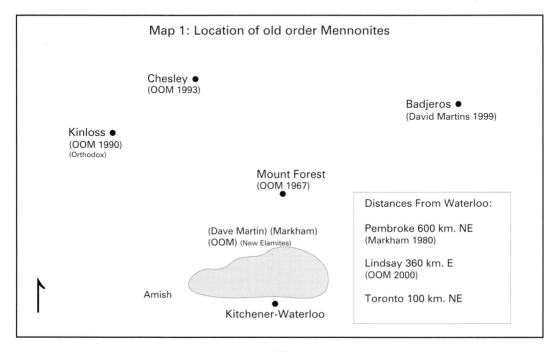

Map 1: Location of old order Mennonites

Chesley ●
(OOM 1993)

Badjeros ●
(David Martins 1999)

Kinloss ●
(OOM 1990)
(Orthodox)

Mount Forest
(OOM 1967)
●

(Dave Martin) (Markham)
(OOM) (New Elamites)

Amish

●
Kitchener-Waterloo

Distances From Waterloo:

Pembroke 600 km. NE
(Markham 1980)

Lindsay 360 km. E
(OOM 2000)

Toronto 100 km. NE

recently two smaller communities exist at considerable distance from the larger centres. In 1999 some of the David Martin group moved to the Maxwell-Badjeros (180 km. north of Waterloo) area. In 2000 a few farmers of the Old Order Mennonites moved just east of Lindsay (360 km. northeast of Waterloo). Over the past forty years a few families have attempted to start new districts, but have been unsuccessful. Eventually they moved back to more populated old order communities. These folk cannot sustain their lifestyle unless they are sufficient in number to form a community in which interdependence in all aspects of life is practised.

Old order Mennonites are not a cohesive group. From 1889 several divisions have occurred in their history. Most splinter groups carry the name of their original leader. The original old order Mennonite group is registered as Old Order Mennonite, and has a population larger than the other groups put together. In this book the author is describing this larger group with a present population of about fifty-eight hundred. For this group I use the designation of OOMs. When referring to the old order Mennonites in general, I do not use capital lettering. Specific smaller groups are identified by name.

As residents in and around the area where old orders live, rural and urban people purchase their garden produce or maple syrup at the farmers' market. We quickly pass their horse and buggy by car on county roads. We see a few farmers till their land with a team or two of horses. As tourists we are invited to visit St. Jacobs or Elmira, viewing pamphlets displaying a Mennonite barn-raising, or women in traditional dress, quilting. We are drawn to artists who paint or photograph this traditional life. In our desire to see and learn more, a few of us make an effort to speak with them, and find them rather reserved, and somewhat hesitant to engage in dialogue beyond a few sentences. They avoid our cameras. They have chosen a lifestyle which we do not understand. In reading this book we make an attempt, a glimpse, at understanding their simplicity and separateness.

For the public, the distinct mark of the old orders is their use of the horse and buggy. Why do they do this, we ask? The answers will vary, with some saying: "The old ways are good," or "The Bible teaches us to be peculiar," or "Cars carry us too far too quickly." As a direct response a grandparent responded, "For the sake of our young people. With a car they could easily get involved in unwholesome things. It is the same with our wearing the clothing we do."

Various Groups
Colours in the Quilt

In this book reference to Old Order Mennonites is to the group who took the more conservative stance in the 1889 division. They are officially known as Old Order Mennonites, and today are the most populous. Their belief and community lifestyle is fairly much the same, with some changes due to an ever-changing social, political, and economic environment. In the more than 110 years since their origin, there have been several more divisions. The groups described below could also be considered old orders, since they represent variations on an old order theme. They differ in practice, and only slightly in belief. Their common belief rests in a strong tie to tradition and to being separate from, and fairly uncompromising to, the world.

The Markham Group

The largest split occurred in 1939 because of a step into modernity. About a third of the group felt adopting the automobile and telephone would not alter their religious and community life. (This same division had already taken place amongst their counterparts in the United States.) In Canada, this more liberal group lived in the Markham region (about 80 km. north of Toronto) and had periodic contact with the Waterloo group. When they officially separated, a large number in the Waterloo area joined them. With the adoption of cars, trucks, and in recent years vans, vehicles had to be black with the chrome bumpers painted black. This group was identified by outsiders as the Black Bumper Mennonites. Their theology is virtually the same as the parent group, with the exception of car and telephone use. A number of older adults have siblings in the OOM group, and they remain friends. They are officially known as the Markham-Waterloo Mennonite Conference, and refer to themselves as Markhamers. Some serve as van-drivers for horse and buggy groups. Together with the Old Order Mennonites, they operate an extensive parochial school program. Where they live in close proximity, they rotate the use of their Sunday meetingplace.

One may debate whether the Markham group are rightfully classified as old orders. Their roots are the same. People over forty speak the dialect common to old orders. Their church government and form of Sunday service is the same. They are rural and their social life restricts them from mixing with outsiders. Their dress is distinct, though somewhat more liberal than OOMs. Women wear a head covering. Youth find recreation within the community. Markham people differ from OOMs in their means of transportation (cars, vans, and trucks), and have larger farms and machinery. In business the Markham group have more contact with the outside world. Some work for employers outside their community, more modern than themselves. Their church shifted to English about a generation ago, in part because some marriage partners from the United States could not speak the dialect. Their use of cars allows them to travel greater distances, and to have their community spread over a larger geographical area. They now have eleven congregations and 1,332 members. Their sixty-year-plus history shows them to be peculiar by general standards. This peculiarity may evaporate after another decade, with fewer close relatives and fewer links with the "mother" group.

The David Martins

The first break among the Ontario old orders came in 1917. A deacon, and then a minister, both with the name of David Martin, felt church rules should be followed more rigorously. Forty-eight members broke from the original group. They observe a more severe method of ostracising those who do not adhere to church practices. To give an extreme example, a member has only limited contact with a person who has been disciplined by the church. This includes one's spouse or son. A David Martin member is forbidden from attending the funeral of a spouse or son officiated in another church. In 1957 this governing church body moved itself further from the OOMs by having its membership refrain from discussing religion with others. Some were persuaded to leave the group in such dialogues. Since that time there has been minimal interaction between the two. Initially the OOMs referred to them as the "New Borns," and now, more commonly, as "the Daves."

Outsiders find the David Martin way of life the most difficult to comprehend. In many ways they are more conservative than the OOMs. They do not use tractors

on their farms, only horses. They do not use bicycles. Their buggies for Sunday travel have wheels with steel rims, rather than hard rubber like the OOMs (Both the bicycle and steel-rimmed wheels were issues in 1917). Up until the early 1980s, when they required more distant travel they went by bus, train or taxi, and did not hire a neighbour with car or van. Their electricity does not come from the public hydro system, but rather from their own generators. There is, however, a more liberal lifestyle. Children's clothing is a bit more colourful. Children attend public schools. A number of men smoke. Their "cottage industry" of numerous shops which dot the rural landscape produce metal, wood, pipes and plastic. Most are small, with two or three workers. Larger shops operate by robot and computer, and include the production of car parts. This group participates in the government pension plan and in health benefits. Socially they are more distant from society than the larger OOM group. Despite the ban on talk about religion, a number of OOMs find employment in their shops. They now have about 350 families and five meeting houses. They function without a bishop.

Three Smaller Groups

In 1957, Elam Martin, a preacher in the David Martin group, took issue over the strict church rule of excommunication and the autocratic position of the bishop's office. In 1958 another small group from the David Martin people joined them, and about forty members joined in communion. In 1967 one more small group from the OOMs joined them. They incorporated as the Orthodox Mennonites. In 1974, fifty-seven percent of the membership fractured over the issue of the beard and mode of courtship. The larger group were identified as Hoovers, after their minister. In 1987 the Hoovers shifted reluctantly to the David Martin group, and a few back to the Orthodox.

The Orthodox Mennonites observe a very simple lifestyle. They have no electricity, no phones, no running water, and no flush toilets. Horses, rather than tractors, are used for farming. Men grow beards. In the eighties, some of the OOMs sensed a drift away from their ways of the past, and wanted to preserve a more simple lifestyle. Feeling uneasy, a number of families moved to the area of the Orthodox, and some eventually joined this group formally. The Orthodox population expanded considerably. They now have three meeting houses, over 120 families, and operate six schools.

The remnant Elam group is now referred to as the "New" Elam Martin group. It is comprised of about twenty adult members. Their children attend the local school of the OOMs. They speak openly about their faith. All three of the above factions will not attend a church service where their minister is not preaching.

Old Order Mennonites–The Larger Group

Old Order Mennonites now have eighteen congregations and number almost fifty-eight hundred. At the time of their separation from the modern Mennonites in 1889 they resided in the Waterloo and Peel regions, and have branched out to other areas in their search for affordable land.

The first expansion was to the Mount Forest region in 1967. The Mount Forest population now has four meeting houses, five deacons, four preachers and one bishop. Families began moving north of Mount Forest, to the Chesley area in 1993. About 1990 a number of families shifted west of Waterloo and Peel, to the Kinloss area. Chesley and Kinloss now have meeting houses. In 2000 three families from Mount Forest moved about two hundred kilometres east to the Lindsay area. Two years later two more families joined them. The move to a new region is precipitated by insufficient land for farming and inflated land prices. Usually the move is made by a family with two or three sons soon to begin farming. It is not a strategically planned endeavour by the church. Periodically such ventures flounder, in that other families do not follow. After about six years, should the numbers not show promise to warrant a church community, the small group are likely to sell their farms and return to one of the existing communities.

IV

Belief

Committed to Tradition, One Another, and God

Theology

What lies behind the traditional dress of the old orders, the use of smaller and older implements, travel by horse and buggy, the persistence in using their own dialect, and their resistance to what is modern? These questions can only be answered by understanding their belief.

The key word in this theological search is *Gelassenheit*. It refers to a submission and a yielding to one another. The qualities of humility, servanthood, tolerance and patience are all found in Gelassenheit. The end result is community. This stands at the opposite pole to individualism, personal goals, pride and individual rights. Submission and yielding is found in every sphere of old order life: child to parent, youth to adult, female to male, person to group, family to the church and laity to clergy. It is a very serious offense for one to criticize decisions made by the clergy.

Final authority is given to those chosen through the church as leaders. The ministerial consists of deacons, ministers and bishops. The basis of their faith is the literal interpretation of the Lutheran German version of the Bible. Its understanding is found in the Dortrecht Confession, first printed in Holland in 1632, and in English in America in 1725. Mennonites accepted this Confession in Kitchener in 1841.

The beliefs of the church are found in the eighteen articles of faith. They address such issues as God, the afterlife, communion, marriage, love, submission to the community, obedience, and surrender. All youth who wish to become church members are catechized in these articles. This is followed by a solemn rite of baptism and church membership. Seventy to one hundred new members observe this ritual annually.

The practice of the church is found in the *Ordnung*, or order of the church. This serves as the rule book. Specific behaviours fall into two categories, either forbidden or strongly discouraged. For example, smoking is forbidden and fishing trips are strongly discouraged. This list of rules does change through group discussion twice annually. On a specified Sunday, adults in groups speak with two or three ministers and a bishop, indicating their being prepared for communion. They will also voice concerns they have about the community. After all the council meetings have taken place, the ministry meet on the Friday before the first communion Sunday. They decide whether changes will be made. These counsel sessions are not meant to voice complaints about another person. Should this occur, the complainant is asked whether he or she has privately voiced their concern with that specific member (Matthew 18:15-20). The process does have a distinct democratic flavour, but the ultimate decisions remain with the ministers. Old and new rules are read after the communion service.

The Ordnung, or book of rules, functions to keep community, to perpetuate the good aspects of tradition, and to foster a God-pleasing life. Most aspects of the larger world are seen as evil. Modernity is a move away from the good of the past. Fashion, the hectic pace of modern life, advertising, the dirty side of politics, and the ruthless pursuit of money are part of this worldly system. Therefore old orders seek to be separate. There is a lot of emphasis placed upon being humble. Pride may show itself in multiple ways: house decorations and furniture, financial achievement, understanding of the Bible, vigour in sports, physical prowess, or arguments. Lack of submission may be evident in one's relation to parents, adults, the ministry, or the ideals of the community.

Another community value is work, particularly physical work. Work is a gift from God. Children are taught to work, and not complain. Given the value of work, efficiency and the use of modern tools are viewed with much caution. At the same time, on an individual basis, the one who can invent ways to reduce work and strenuous labour within the context of the old order lifestyle is respected. However, lest pride arise, little fuss is made over such innovation. Leisure invites activity which is suspect, and thus should be used to complement the community, and not the self, nor should it be costly. The primary leisure activity is visitation, particularly on Sunday. This activity is strongly endorsed. A restful family time in the evening, possibly with games or reading, is common. Daytime quilting bees by young or older women are also endorsed. Group singing is a wholesome activity. Recreation filled with competition and argument is not conducive to Gelassenheit, nor good Christian character.

Prized virtues in the outside community, such as self esteem and a good self concept, are rejected. One thinks in terms of others, and ideally places the family and community ahead of oneself. It may appear that one is always open for some violation. Any act that is perceived as against the community is seen as a wrongdoing before God. Any such behaviour must show repentance and confession. With this confession one is reinstated as a full member of the community.

OOMs feel they are faithful to God, not because of their clothing or horse and buggy, but because of a much larger core of values and behaviours based on their tradition and the Bible. In brief, these qualities include simplicity, humility, Gelassenheit, non-resistance, non-conformity to the world, and a willingness to suffer for faith.

Rules

Some topics often surface in the biannual counsel meetings. Dress is one example, and the size of farm implements is another. At one point tractors could not be used in the barn, because their upward directed exhaust could ignite a fire. With horizontal and lower exhaust pipes, this rule was lifted. Farmers may not use self-propelled combines, but they may hire someone to do this form of combining. The same principle holds true for large-roll hay-balers. The use of telephones in the home was discussed more than a decade before it was adopted in 1989. Concerns centred upon: Is this aspect of modernity necessary? Will it be misused by youth? Will people gossip? The debate was complex, because phones were being used for business purposes in many shops and some barns. A very small number said they needed the phone in the home for health reasons. Furthermore, some used their neighbours' phones, and such a practice appeared inconsistent to some.

The rules of this community would undoubtedly be seen as rather restrictive by outsiders. Dress stipulations include length, style and colour of dress, colour and style of shirt, trousers, cap and hat, and style of shoe. Clothes dryers, wall-to-wall rugs, radios, microwaves, television and telephone answering machines are forbidden. Excessively large mirrors and fancy decorative china cabinets are forbidden, as well as ornamentation and artificial flowers inside or outside the house. Tractors are not to have more than one hundred horsepower. Lightning rods on buildings are forbidden because one is to put total faith in God. One is discouraged from using tractor lights and working late into the night. At one time liquid manure tanks were forbidden, but are now accepted. Covered buggies have a specified window size. This evolved from a member installing a car window that could open and close, which was ruled as vain. The rule against windshields on covered buggies was lifted a number of years ago. Rules forbid the use of cowboy clothes, wrist watches, rings, and cameras.

Whatever the society, some rules will appear restrictive, unfair or inappropriate in some particular situations. Here is one example within this community, at least as seen by an outsider. One may use the tractor and wagon for haulage on one's property, but not on public roads, other than where one's farmland is adjacent to the road. Therefore one is not permitted to haul hay purchased from a neighbour a kilometre down the road. Even if it is eight o'clock at night, and one has a half load of hay remaining, and it might rain during the night, one is to return to the farm with one's tractor. One cannot tow the wagon with baled hay. The principle is to restrict the use of the tractor in road transportation, and encourage the use of horses to haul the hay. At this time, OOM farmers have horses for buggy use, but few large Clydesdales or Percherons for such haulage.

Change

It may appear to outsiders that this segment of the Canadian mosaic is locked into the time frame of the very early industrialization period. This is not the case. There is change, and leaders of the community are quite aware of it. They seek to manage change to the advantage of the entire community. Change operates at a different pace from our own, and it also emerges from a very different set of values.

As with any group of people, change is stimulated by a number of sources. Individuals find they can preform a task with greater efficiency by adopting some new device. OOMs may purchase, invent, or adapt a tool which will reduce the time and energy involved in production. Such a practice may be yet uncharted and undefined in terms of church rules, while new visions push prescribed boundaries. Possibly the margin is somewhat vague, and allows for experimentation. Every social group, whether conservative or liberal, has a boundary or edge. In every social group a few or many, literally live "on the edge," and this edge is continually redefined. Among OOMs this consideration may be related to production, furniture, or ornamentation of vehicles, buildings, or oneself. In some cases, only after someone dares the "trial run" is the activity ruled as acceptable or unacceptable. This is true of a thought or idea, even one that impacts religious belief. New circumstances may question long-held practices. OOM rules prescribe three categories: the accepted, the forbidden, and what is "strongly discouraged." With time the latter category may shift to the forbidden, or to the accepted, category. The tolerance of telephones in the home is one such example.

Older people have seen change in their lifetimes. Very few children in the OOM group now attend public schools. Children are less compelled to do farmwork after school than they were a generation earlier. Our society has better methods of health care. Sanitation rules for the barn and livestock are much more strict, and butchering practices are carefully monitored by the government. OOMs have adopted these standards. As an example, there is now no home-butchering where the meat is sold. The selling of farm stock has been streamlined in that truckers now come to the farmyard weekly for cattle and hogs, and when appropriate for chickens. The face of the free market system has changed radically. Corporations and government have a much greater bearing on market fluctuations. One example is the use of quota for cows and poultry. Again, farmers have adapted.

Change in the larger society is fostered by television, radio and the printed media, and for children, to some degree, by classmates. Retailers target a specific age group, and underscore popular appeal and prestige. These means do not apply to OOMs. There is, however, a recognized and institutional means of change among the OOMs. They hold biannual meetings where the past and present are reviewed.

This relates to theological as well as practical aspects of everyday life. These council meetings are always held before the biannual communion meetings, and are treated with gravity. On the specified Sunday both male and female members have the option to enter the council room in the meeting house in groups and voice their feelings about the ebb and flow of the community to the preacher, deacon, and bishop. Some voice their concerns and affirmations during the year within informal settings. Change is controlled principally by the chosen ministerial, and to a lesser degree, the men over fifty-five.

V Church

Keeping the Holy Day in Community

Meetingplace

The word "meetingplace" is a translation from the German *Versamlung Haus*. The word "church" is seldom used. The church yard consists of three distinct areas, the meeting house, "parking" for horses and buggies, and cemetery. The parking area has heavy posts fixed in the ground, linked by chain, to which horses are tied. White-painted, non-flushing toilets for males are also located here. Cemeteries increase in size with the age of the congregation. Tombstones are simple. Married couples are interred beside one another. Should an individual die by suicide he is buried at the edge of the cemetery.

A local member serves as caretaker. For his paid services he keeps the yard and building clean, and on colder days, will light the heaters on Saturday evening. When the meetinghouse has an unusually large crowd, he arranges benches in an accommodating manner. Annual cleaning and, if necessary, painting are done by community members, mostly women, on one day in the spring. The deacon or local caretaker will be in charge of this event, and the choice to assist is totally voluntary. Larger repair jobs are done by men.

The meeting house is rectangular and constructed of wood (white) or brick (brown) by volunteer work of local and more distant members. Most measure about fifteen by twenty-five metres, the larger ones seating 250 people. Costs of building materials are paid by the entire membership. There are two entrances for males: one at the end for married men, one on the long side of the building for male youth. A second entrance is for female youth, which opens to the women's cloak room. Two more entrances, one for women with children, the other for older women, are located on the other end of the building. Each of these last two entrances opens to a room in which women hang their bonnets and coats. Adjacent to the older women's room is a toilet and sink. In these cloakrooms women hang their bonnets and coats and tend to the needs of young children during the service. The older women's room doubles as a council room when required.

In the large meeting space a long bench, upon which deacons, preachers and the bishop sit, is located on one of the longer sides of the structure. Just in front of them is a pulpit, elevated one step off the floor, from which the minister preaches. No microphone is used. Electricity is not required because there are no evening meetings. The rest of the building has crude benches without cushions. One is impressed with the distinct arrangement of women on one side, men on the other. Within this division, there are specific areas for older men, older women, younger married men, women with children, male youth and female youth (in the centre), and boys and girls (near the front). Above the men are wood appendages from the

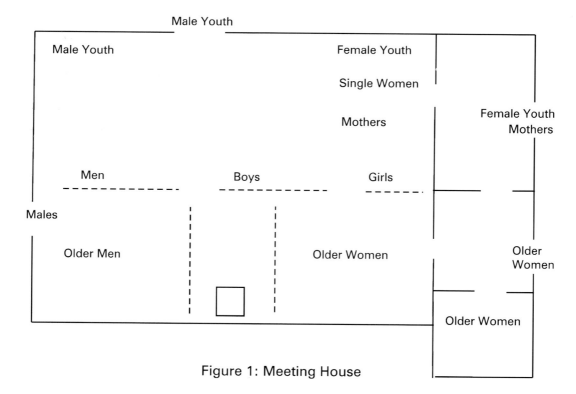

Figure 1: Meeting House

ceiling, with wood pegs upon which men hang their hats. Several large vents, each controlled with a cord, extend through the roof to facilitate temperature control. An oil or gas stove with a long running pipe obstructs the rows of benches. A second stove is located in the women's room. Benches are set on at least three tiers, ascending toward the back. Simple sliding sash windows may be opened as required. The structure contains no cross, icons, pictures, wood ornamentation, or stained glass windows.

Sunday Gatherings

Sunday services normally begin at 10:00 a.m, half an hour earlier on special occasions such as council or communion. Male youth generally enter en masse just about the time the meeting is to begin. It lasts for about two hours, depending on the length of the sermons. Outsiders seldom attend, though they are welcome. On such occasions the preacher will adapt, using English for part of his sermon. The small, black, German hymn book without music is located in the rack in the back of the bench, just ahead of where one sits. There are no musical instruments, all singing is in unison, and the pace is slow. Each hymn is begun by a *Vorsinger* (song leader). He chooses the correct tune and pitch, begins singing the first line, and the congregation immediately follows on the second beat or the second word. This holds true for each stanza.

Children sit remarkably quietly throughout the service. On very rare occasions a boy misbehaves. If he is quite young, his father will take him outside, or come and sit next to him. Should some male youth create a disturbance, an adult is likely to make his way to sit amongst them. Periodically a child or adult leaves for the outside toilet, or a parent walks out with a crying child. These aberrations are noted by all. Such movements along seated pews is extremely difficult, due to the space. The order of service is predictable.

Table 1. Sunday Order of Service

Hymn: Initiated by one of the two song leaders

Scripture text: Read by the visiting deacon. The sermon is based upon this reading

Opening sermon: Generally for twenty to twenty-five minutes by the local minister

Silent prayer: All kneel

Main sermon: Forty-five to sixty minutes duration, by the visiting minister.

Testimonies: Deacons briefly affirm that what they have heard is consistent
 with Scripture
Vocal prayer: All kneel, while the minister offers an audible prayer
Closing Hymn: Chosen by the song leader
Benediction: Given by the one who has preached the main sermon

The audible prayer, given by the preacher of the main sermon, invariably includes gratitude for being able to assemble for worship, prayer for the government, the sick, food and "raiment" (clothing). At times the prayer may include guidance for those who visit the sick, or for a cessation of rain during harvest. The prayer does not include any specific person's, or family's, need, such as illness or bereavement. At the time of prayer there is a general rumble, while all people turn around, kneeling with their folded hands upon the bench they have been seated on.

There may be an announcement or two, but this is rare. No church offering is taken during the service itself. On a non-Sunday service like Good Friday, members have the option of using the offering box hung inside the church, at the doors. One may also leave a donation with the deacon during the week at the church or his home, at designated times. Every family is familiar with the annual cycle of church collections, and the amount each congregation is expected to give. Collections are made for expenses relating to the church, such as the custodian's salary and heating, the poor and needy of the membership, twice annually for the school system, health expenses of the membership, and one annual offering for those outside the membership such as the needy abroad. Other collections are taken when required, to cover expenses when a member's farm building or house is burned, or, even more rarely, expenses to pay monies levied by an outsider due to an accident.

Annual Church Events

Communion is held in April and September. It is preceded by an important Sunday of self-examination. The tone for these events is a humble and submissive relationship with God, which is evident by a right relationship with all in the church community. The sermon is on the chapter of Matthew 18 where Jesus admonishes his disciples to live sensitively with one another. The service is succeeded by its members going into the preacher's room in groups of nine to thirteen males, then females, and voicing their affirmation of the church community. These groups are usually the older of the congregation, though they are open to the full membership. Individuals may indicate concerns regarding the preservation of the community, or the loosening of some practices. This is the democratic forum of the community. Concerns that arise are the use or abuse of the telephone, size of farm equipment, the dress code, and the re-acceptance of a once-deviant member. During the week the clergy meet to discuss comments that have been made, as well as direction they deem appropriate for the future. This week is known as *Umfrage* or council meetings.

The following Sunday all meet for communion at 9:30 a.m. All members partake of the bread (body of Christ), and wine (blood of Christ). Children are then dismissed from the service. This is followed by the ritual of foot-washing, showing submission to one another. In groups of two, man with man and woman with woman, each "wash" the other's feet, following Jesus' example (John 13:5-17). Men engage in foot-washing in the auditorium and the women in the cloakroom. This communion service is the most central service of the community. At the conclusion of the service, the bishop reads all the rules of the church, including any new resolutions.

It is significant that any change in the community occurs with the pivotal religious event of communion. Its importance is reinforced when a person misses three consecutive communions and is no longer considered a member. Communion Sunday is also marked in that it takes three Sundays before all districts have observed it. Other events mentioned below are observed one day only. The one exception is baptism, which is clustered in two Sundays in about one half of all the districts.

The second important annual church event is Easter. Another highlight is baptism, held in late July and early August, when new members, who have had six weeks of instruction, are received into the church. This instruction lasts for two and a half hours on Sunday afternoons. Membership candidates are expected to attend both the morning and afternoon services. These sessions are also attended by children and families of the baptismal candidates, as well as others. Prospective members sit up at the front. Generally clusters of three churches gather for this purpose. The usual Sunday morning service in not as full in attendance while these membership meetings are held.

Another service which occurs annually is Pentecost (the descent of the Holy Spirit), on the seventh Sunday after Easter. Other significant church events not restricted to Sunday, are Christmas, Thanksgiving (the first Thursday preceding the first Friday in September), and Ascension (forty days after Easter).

Sunday Observance

Sundays are holy days in which only essential work, such as farm chores and duties for food preparation, is done. No farmer will harvest his hay crop on Sunday, even if rain appears imminent. During maple syrup running time, work is terminated from midnight to midnight, though tree taps are left to drip. When a church service is held during a weekday, such as on Christmas, the sabbath restriction of work does not apply. Some may visit in the afternoon, and others return to farm work.

Another custom closely linked to Sunday is visiting. Church meetings are staggered so that virtually every second Sunday fifty percent of the districts have no service. Families are encouraged to visit churches in other districts, but are not obligated. It is a common valued practice to visit some family in the district in which a service is being held. Families in the district expect visitors, and take pleasure in hosting such events with well-prepared meals. A large noon meal is served, and a light lunch in the afternoon. Often families return home for evening chores, though some may visit a second family for supper. Youth often hang around longer. Sunday dress is worn until they return home. Youth also meet on Sunday evenings for singings. Youth are not to become involved in competitive sports, and Sunday clothes are not to be changed for more vigorous play activity. Visiting is the pinnacle of leisure activity, and is strongly reinforced by the church leadership.

VI

Election of Ministers
And the Lot Falls on ...

No other event grips the old order community as much as the selection of a deacon, preacher, or bishop. The spirit of community is strongly reinforced. A leader is chosen under the guidance of God, and will have a significant influence upon the entire group for the remainder of his life. A minister is chosen in one of the following situations: a local minister has died, is elderly and incapable of continuing the service, or has been banned (a rare event); a new district has been formed; or a congregation has expanded, requiring assistance. This leader is male. At baptism every male makes the promise that he will serve in ministry, should he be chosen. Similarly, women affirm that in the future, should their husband be chosen as minister, she will faithfully do her part in this sacred role. The choice for these three sacred offices is made with very little human involvement. It is a process not generally found in Christian churches, where persons enter the ministry because of a personal call, seminary training, or through a democratic vote in a congregation. Amongst old orders, a minister is chosen through the random selection of a book, among several, one of which has a significant paper in it. This method, know as selection by "lot," was used to select the twelve disciples after Jesus' ascension (Acts 1:26).

After a Sunday morning service and sermon, on the designated day, the bishop and local minister and/or deacon meet in the council room to hear members' "votes" (suggestions) for the role to be filled (deacon or preacher). In the case of selecting a bishop, "voting" takes place on two Sundays in the districts which this bishop will represent. While all may engage in this voting, in practice only men, particularly those over about age forty-five, do. In newer congregations the age is lower. Unless the presiding ministers do not approve of the presented names, which is rarely the case, all are presented to the congregation that same morning. There is a hush within the congregation as names are presented. That afternoon the phone lines are busy, giving this information to residents in other districts.

Candidates for preacher can range in age from twenty-two to forty-six. Deacon candidates are rarely in their twenties, due to the responsibility and nature of their role. Bishops are chosen from among preachers. There is a general understanding that bishop candidates must have served as minister for at least two years. "Voted" members are usually married. Young men have been voted while single, and in one case a single man was selected; however, that individual had already made plans for marriage. All clergy serve without remuneration, though food gifts and service will be given by individuals. The afternoon after the day of the vote (Monday), all the candidates and their wives meet at church with most of the ordained leaders present. Though all gave evidence of willingness to serve in this capacity, at the time of baptism, each of the voted men and their wives are asked again regarding this commitment. They are then instructed in this new role.

On Tuesday the pivotal event takes place. One of the voted candidates will be selected by lot. The meeting place is filled to over capacity half an hour before the scheduled starting time. All the ministers from the Ontario districts are present. Several ministers from the U.S., including a bishop, are likely to be present. Many from neighbouring districts refrain from attending, simply because of limited space. Close relatives of voted members from other districts are all present. The local bishop presides. The voted candidates sit according to chronological age on the benches in front of the table from which sermons are preached. Their wives sit in this same order on the front "older women's" bench.

A number of identical hymn books equal to the number of voted candidates lie on the front table. In one of these books will be put a paper which reads, "The lot is cast into the lap; but the whole disposing thereof is of the Lord" (Proverbs 16:33). Whoever selects this book is the one chosen as deacon, preacher, or bishop. Hymns and prayers are made, and at least two sermons are preached. Two deacons gather the special books and go into the council room where the books are mixed. They return and set the books on end on the table. The bishop may also mix the books one final time. The crowded audience is in a deep, sombre silence as the proceedings continue. The oldest candidate rises from his seat and selects a book, then sits down. The others follow in age sequence. Then the bishop asks for the book from the first man, and searches for the special paper. This process is repeated until the slip of paper is found. This is God's moment. This is God's selection of leadership for this congregation. It is awesome!

There is release and relief once the appropriate book is selected. With the choice complete, the bishop has the candidate kneel on the pulpit step, lays his hands on him and ordains him. The two exchange a handshake, and the bishop gives him a holy kiss. A few of the other ministers follow with the holy kiss and a few words of spiritual encouragement. A hymn is sung, and the other clergymen from the ministers' bench will offer their spiritual support. With the conclusion of the service, others from the congregation come to offer the selected one and his wife best wishes. The selected man is conscious of his responsibility before God and his people. He is a marked man. He receives high respect because of his role in the brotherhood. The membership are not to speak negatively of the decisions of their ministers. This man's decisions (under God) will affect the direction of these people, and, in some cases, the lives of individuals. Members know that they are impacted, to some degree, by the personalities of these men, by their generosity and severity, their rigidity and flexibility, as well as their disposition for change.

If the selection is for preacher, the Sunday after the selection he reads the Scripture found in I Corinthians 13, a chapter on love, in a meeting, and soon thereafter will speak for ten to fifteen minutes, and eventually more completely fill the preacher role. His family, business and social life is to be a Christian example, setting the standard for conservative behaviour and dress. For almost all of the twentieth century, selected ministers and deacons "downgraded" conveniences, removing the telephone and electricity from their homes and farms. Out with electric lights, stove, freezer, and refrigerator. Rubber-tired tractors were changed to steel wheels with hard rubber rims. Through the nineties there was a general sentiment that such a change for a farmer was not justifiable, given that he had used electricity in the normal functions on his farm all his life, some for almost three decades. One's daily attitude and behaviour should be the model! In 1999 electricity was permitted for elected clergy, though the ownership of the telephone inside the house was strongly discouraged.[1] On church meeting days, clergy wear a cape rather than a conventional coat, as well as more traditional trousers.

---

[1] Before 1999 inequity between clergymen was fairly pronounced. Clergymen who lived near or adjacent to one of their children's homes had easy access to a phone and even an electric freezer. Other ministers did not have these amenities.

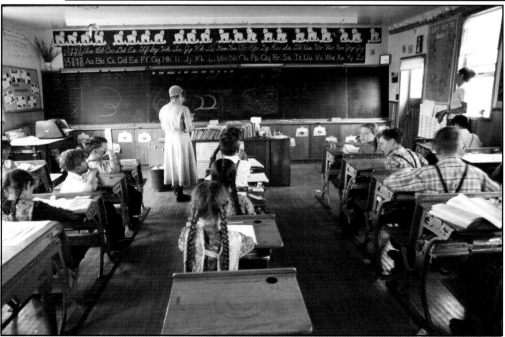

44

VII Family
We Lead Our Children by Example

Activity

While there is variation in the OOM family, it is not as vast as in the larger Canadian society. This OOM population is all rural. No one has more than a grade eight education. Their means of transportation is horse, buggy, bicycle, and walking. Families are generally larger, with five to ten children in completed families. Thus there is a lot of sibling interaction, and these folk are also more apt to have contact with grandparents, uncles, aunts, and cousins. There are no solo parents, except for widows and widowers whose children interact with extended family members. Their schools are less than two kilometres distance and comprised of children from their church group, as well as from the Markham group.

The family setting is the farmyard. This includes the home, at least one barn with animals, at least one shed for machinery and buggies, possibly a shop, a large garden with fruit trees, and a lawn area on which to play. Children have wagons, bikes, and swings, the latter likely in the yard as well as long hanging ropes in the hay loft. The sandbox is filled with farm implements and even trucks. Children are familiar with a variety of domesticated animals, knowing how to give them proper care. Older children observe the birthing of farm animals. Children play with the farmyard dogs and cats. A child's mother is always nearby, and the father not too far away, readily

accessible for protection, care and discipline. Some fathers choose to work at home on the farm, rather than at a day job, simply to be among their family. Meals are eaten together. The father works into the evening on the farmyard, while his wife continues the endless tasks in the kitchen. Children are also in the kitchen, helping, doing homework or playing games. Older children and adults may be reading one of three magazines, *Blackboard Bulletin*, *Family Life* or *Young Companion*, published by the Amish. They delight in servings of popcorn in the evening.

The house is plain. The basement has hundreds of canned jars from the garden and at least one freezer full of food. The upstairs has several bedrooms. There may

be one to four children in a room. Each bedroom has a closet, small compared to those in other Canadian homes, and a chest of drawers for clothing. There may be an additional room for guests or for quilting. The parents' bedroom may be on the main floor or upstairs. The top floor is warmed by means of vents in the ceiling with heat coming from the kitchen wood stove or the furnace in the basement.

The house is commonly entered by means of a hallway, where one may place clothes and caps on hooks and boots on the floor. Adjacent, and at times in combination, is the clothes-washing room which has a separate small door where one may hang clothes on the clothesline extending to the outside. The washer, spin dryer and sink are the main furnishings here–no dryer!

The other rooms on this floor are kitchen, living room and three-piece bathroom. No pictures adorn the walls, except for a few calendars. These calendars have pictures of animals or of scenery. The living room, where men meet when there is company, is smaller than the kitchen. It has a couch, sturdy wood chairs, and a table. On a

bureau (and also in the kitchen) is a chime clock, dinging rhythmically the half hour. Some are heirlooms. A few house plants hang near the windows. A china cabinet, likely constructed by one of the many Mennonite cabinet-makers, is the most decorative item in the house, complete with china. This room may also serve

as a sewing room or a place to host quilting bees.

The kitchen is the primary room of the house, where one prepares meals, eats, does any necessary book work, telephones, and entertains. In winter it is likely the only really warm room in the house. The large wood table seats ten people, with leaves to accommodate many more. A sturdy bench and chairs grace its sides. Appliances include an electric and wood stove, refrigerator, and food mixer, but not a microwave. The wood stove has a rectangle of sturdy wood dowels near the ceiling where clothes hang to dry. In summer only the electric stove is used. A calendar with scenic pastoral pictures or animals may hang on the wall. Near the outside entrance is a sink with a small mirror,

used by those coming in from farm work.

Transportation is essential for every old order. Standard equipment for every household is a horse and buggy. A road horse costs between fifteen and twenty-five hundred dollars. Virtually all these horses have proven to be unfit in one of the local racetracks. They are often about five years old, and are good for the road for another eight years. Horses have different qualities, such as impatience, nervousness, slowness, speed, orneriness, gentleness, and endurance. When they are no longer road-worthy, they may be sold as meat for eight hundred dollars. One faces a risk in purchasing a horse. Most are purchased from a local horse-trader, which may include OOMs. The stereotype of the horse-trader is applicable. Were one to purchase the feed and bedding, as the few who live in villages must, the cost is fifteen dollars weekly. One tends to the hooves at the blacksmith every eight weeks at a cost of twenty to fifty dollars. An open buggy costs about thirty-five hundred dollars, and the smallest covered one a minimum of four thousand (a larger one up to fifty-five hundred). The hard rubber around the rim of the wheels must be replaced every three to five years. Interestingly, elderly men unable to drive a horse face the same psychological predicament as those in the larger society who are unable to drive a car.

Primary Events

a. Weddings

Weddings are unmistakeably a community highlight. The couple take great pride in keeping the date of the wedding secret until three weeks prior, when the fact is made public with the publishing of banns at church. Usually the couple are not in church that day. A few people may have become suspicious earlier because of evident

wedding preparations, like the painting of the fence in the yard where the wedding is to be held, generally in the bride's home. The bishop is asked regarding an appropriate date some four months in advance. He seeks to avoid two weddings on the same day in all eighteen districts. Weddings are preferably held on a Wednesday, but may take place on Thursday or Tuesday. This allows time so that activity both before and after the wedding will not impact a Sunday. Almost all first marriages are held in June, July, or August, after seeding and before harvesting. However the weddings of widows and widowers tend to be spread throughout the year.

Before the event the couple will personally deliver invitations to a carefully selected 120-30 people. Before the eighties guests numbered about eighty, and each household received a personally written invitation. Now photocopies are made. Guests include the immediate family of the bridal couple, grandparents, a selected few aunts, uncles and cousins, and close friends of the bride and groom. Since no one attends unless specially invited, every guest feels thrilled and honoured to be present.

The weeks before the event are spent in food preparation, program, and thoroughly cleaning the house and yard. The wedding is almost always a full-day event, beginning at 9:00 a.m. Young men aged sixteen to eighteen, known as "hostlers," meet the guests, and unharness and care for the horses. (Each horse and buggy and owner receive a ticket with a number, so as to facilitate the hook-up at departure time.) Levity pervades here, in that the boys are tipped for their services. Similarly, young women are tipped for their labour in waiting on tables. As the guests enter the house, young married men serve all adults a small glass of wine with a large cookie. This is the only time and place, aside from communion, that wine is permitted in the OOM community.

During the first two hours a solemn service is held, during which time the bishop and preacher admonish the husband and wife of their duties, practical aspects of marriage, and how to live good Christian lives. After the vows the registry is signed. No rings are exchanged, nor an embrace or kiss. The bride wears a dress of dark blue knit material and the groom a navy blue suit of synthetic material, each of which will be worn later as Sunday dress. The nuptial couple sit together, as do all other couples at the wedding. (Weddings and house meetings after funerals are the only times this coupling occurs publicly.) A sumptuous meal follows. The bride decides upon the food to be eaten. It is often scalloped potatoes, or a potato casserole, various salads, one type of meat (ham, chicken or meat balls), plates of cookies and squares, a milk pudding dessert, fruit salad, and a chiffon or layered cake.

In the afternoon youth and children sing songs and play games. Children hand out small baskets of popcorn and oranges to all. Males are expected to pay for the treat. Later the wedded couple hand out trays of candy with a snippet of both the bride and groom's dress and suit. At 4:00 or 4:30 many of the guests leave for home. The "young folks" and immediate relatives of the bride and groom stay for supper and a lighter time of frivolity. A small child may hide the groom's shoe, and the groom pays for its retrieval. Someone may give the couple spoof cutlery such as a tiny spoon and a huge fork! A few activities organized by the bride, such as word and guessing games are played. The newlyweds remain in this home overnight, and the next day travel to their new home by horse and buggy, unless their home is more distant.

All wedding gifts are practical. Newlyweds receive a lot of assistance in gift and in kind from their parents, if they are able. Mother and daughter have already selected an eighteen or twenty-four-piece set of dishes, as well as cutlery, which are used at the wedding. They have preserves of vegetables, fruit, relishes and meat. The bride's parents often provide a wood-burning stove, refrigerator, washing machine, and couch, often bought at an auction sale. This may also include a bedroom suite. Sufficient food for the first two weeks is given by the bride's parents. Her parents also give a cow. The husband already owns a horse, buggy and a few beef cattle or hogs. His family supplies a bed and dresser. If either of their parents are carpenters, they have made some of the furniture, including a kitchen table. Both before and after the wedding kin assist in renovating the house and barn, or possibly the building of a new barn or shed. If the residence is near kin, machinery may be loaned. Such exchange is extensive, and boosts family interdependence. At the wedding, attendants bring gifts which are usually opened (though not among the more conservative families). Some choose to give their gifts later, to avoid duplication and public display.

b. Funerals

Funerals are all-day events, held two or three days after death unless there are non-old order close relatives who live some distance away. A viewing is held in the home of the deceased the day before the funeral. The day of the funeral immediate family members gather at the home for a brief service, then follow the minister's buggy, then the horse-drawn hearse to the church. In the back yard of the meetingplace all attendees view the open casket, while family members stand in an arc a few metres away. After the viewing, the casket is carried to the prepared grave in the church cemetery. Relatives and close friends view the interment. Others make their way into the meeting house. The service reinforces the inevitable fact of death for all, and the need to be prepared to meet God.

After the service all who wish may drive to the home of the deceased for refreshments and conversation. At times there are 140 people in attendance With the death of a parent, that same evening or the day after the funeral, the adult children meet to read the will. Usually all children, regardless of age or gender, receive an equal amount. If there are items that two or more children wish to have, or if the value cannot be amiably agreed upon, it is left for auction. Here the public as well as family members may bid. The community does not want to see disagreement and hard feelings over the division of an estate. In the event of the death of a father with young children, a brother is likely to help in farm management. He may do this for several years, until a teenage son, with guidance from his mother, is able to do the work.

c. Other Events

The birth of a child does carry some excitement, though this is shown differently than in wider circles. Young women in the church district do know who is expecting, and often "compare notes." This is not mentioned publicly because it is a private

matter. With the birth of a child, siblings, grandparents, great grandparents, aunts, uncles, and women in the church district are happy. The latter often visit the new mother and bring a gift. Births are not mentioned in the church, and there is no dedication. Mothers bring their infants to a service after three to five weeks. Birthdays of children may be celebrated with a special cake. No gift is given, nor is "Happy Birthday" sung.

Possibly the cultural value of humility and selflessness squelch an exuberance of excitement and celebration. Children take delight in telling their parents and grandparents of successfully completing a grade in school, and expect a compliment. Similarly, parents are pleased to find that their youth want to join the church. It is common for families with married children to meet all together at least once a year. Larger extended family gatherings take place periodically.

VIII

Youth

For many OOMs over age fifty the greatest concern is for their youth, those between ages fifteen to twenty-three. An elderly man said, "This is the only age when we have no control over them." While youth have some independence, it is minimal compared with the outside society. Serious offenses would be disobedience and lack of respect for parents and church leaders, more likely found in males than females. Conspicuous deviance is hanging out at bars, watching TV and drinking, frequent association with non-old orders, working for a non-Mennonite, smoking, driving a car, owning a tape deck player, or listening to inappropriate music. A common complaint is being too engaged and competitive in sports. Female deviance is seen in dress and hair. The community feels that proper training in a child's more formative years will minimize problems during youth. "Train up a child in the way he should go and when he is old he will not depart from it" (Proverbs 22:6) is a key proverb. Parents are expected to correct faulty behaviour.

OOMs, whether old or young, enjoy singing. Church music is in German, has a slow beat, and only the melody is sung. Amongst themselves, youth sing in English, in four part harmony, and sing a variety of hymns. Youth groups cheer the sick with their songs. Occasionally a group may gather in a silo to sing, and the acoustics permeate the melodic sound throughout the barnyard. They may sing while quilting, or travelling by car or van. Youth meet to swim, play softball, volleyball or hockey, differentiated by gender. In the past youth gathered to husk corn, pull nails from a pile of used lumber, or pick stones from the field of a family who needed help. The latter two events still occasionally take place.

The institutionalized event exclusively for youth is singings. On Sunday nights from seventy-five to 150 youth from possibly three districts gather in a home to sing and have fun. Youth begin attending when they are fifteen. At this age, women

begin to wear their hair up in a bun, and wear a head covering when attending church. Singings have restrictions that are set by adults: the use of the approved English hymnal, no musical instruments, no dancing, no smoking, and no drinking. Almost all are violated to a minor degree. The resident couple of the home are responsible for overseeing the event. They usually remain upstairs. One or two mouth organs are used, an act not viewed as acceptable to the church. Occasionally a radio or tape deck is played outside among a group of males. Singings are not to be held during the six weeks of summer instruction leading to baptism and church membership. Youth terminate singing attendance with marriage, or in their late twenties, whichever occurs first.

Singings begin at 8:00 p.m., boys sitting on one side of the room and girls on the other. A male usually begins each hymn sung in English from a hymnal. They also play a few games. At about 10:00 the fellows with "special friends" go out to hitch their horse to the buggy, then drive around to the front door and make the pick up. The remaining group continue to play games, and in a few cases square dance until midnight. Boys drive their buggies to their girlfriends' homes, which may be eight kilometres away, and visit in the front room, while all other members of the household are asleep. The parents will be aware of this special relationship, and know that there will be visiting in their home late Sunday evening. The boy leaves sometime between 12:00 and 2:00 a.m., driving possibly another eight kilometres to his home. At six the next morning he is in the barn doing the early morning chores.

"Special friend" relationships are initiated by males through letter writing. Extreme care is taken to keep this a secret. Often a sister finds some way to deliver the letter. This correspondence continues for a month or possibly three months, until the horse and buggy pickup is made. These prized times continue after singings, but are augmented with riding together after Sunday services to families' homes for visitation. This courting may continue for sixteen to twenty-four months or more. Eventually they discuss marriage plans with both parents, as well as plans to purchase a farm. Most first-time romances mature to marriage. Compared to our standards of courtship, romance is more controlled, has a closer link to parents and the community, and has a more pragmatic quality.

Those who are widowed, or marry at a later age, have less difficulty with meeting privately. However they also seek to be secretive about their relationship. One man explained that he travelled to Kitchener by bus, and en route his special friend was picked up as well. In the city they joined one another and did a few things together, like going to a restaurant. The courtship of older people is briefer than that of younger people. When I asked a woman why she married a particular widower, she replied, "Who would look after the young children?"

Education
The Little Red School House

IX

For over 165 years OOM children attended their local public schools. In 1964 rural Ontario entered a new era, centralizing schools. This prompted the plain people,

such as the Amish and Mennonites, to initiate their own school program. Local authorities were surprised by this move, because their tax base would be reduced. The challenge for the Mennonites was enormous, given that no one had more than an eighth grade education, and no one had any experience teaching or operating a school system. However, up until this time some parents had served on local public school boards.

Old orders identified several problems with public school centralization. Children would be at a school distant from their homes, with a lengthy time in bus travel. The curriculum had little room for creation and godly teaching. In physical education classes they would be expected to

wear non-modest gym clothes. (Did they not get exercise in walking to school, and doing farm work?) The curriculum would include sex education. The student population would be much more heterogeneous than that found in their rural setting. They would be expected to attend school until age sixteen. With these concerns they initiated letters and meetings with provincial and municipal school officials, and ultimately began their own system.

The school system of the OOMs and Markham group have 1,330 scholars (the term they use) taught by ninety-five teachers and teacher's assistants in forty-five schools and eighty classrooms (2001). There are thirteen one-room, twenty-eight two-room, and three three-room schools, averaging fourteen students per class. Most of the buildings were newly constructed, though some were schools no longer in use due to the decentralization shift. Most are made of wood and painted white, but some fit the stereotype of the little red school house and reflect what was common in Canada in the thirties. As one enters, coats and boots line the cloakroom. Girls wear dresses, and boys wear pants with suspenders. In the early fall and late spring one sees twisting and wiggling bare feet under several desks. At recess and noon hour, virtually all students rush outside, in warm and cold weather, to play tag, softball, prisoner's base, fox and geese, or toboggan. Their play activity has no gender distinction, unlike the public school system, or what they will encounter in their future lives. There are no gymnasiums.

Schools meet for 187 days annually, as required by law. The school year begins the day after Labour Day, as in the public school system. Their "break" occurs at Christmas and Easter. In the spring there are four weeks of half-days for kindergarten children. All teaching is in English, a major transition for most children who exclusively speak their dialect at home. Students recognize the teacher's authority. Students complete the term in which they have their fourteenth birthday. OOM children are not obligated to attend their own parochial school, though about ninety-five per cent do. (All David Martin children attend the public school system.)

Prospective new teachers engage themselves in the classroom for two weeks in the spring, and are tutored in responsibilities. Every summer a two-week course facilitates new and continuing teachers. Throughout the year, senior teachers are designated to assist those newer in the profession. Ninety-three percent of the teachers are female, and thirty-two per cent have had at least ten years of teaching experience. During the year, teachers have three professional development days. Government standard tests from a few decades ago are given annually in all grades.

The curriculum places an emphasis on reading, writing, and arithmetic. Songs of nature and good moral living are sung. A portion of the learning is by memorization. Wall posters show important events in history such as creation, Jesus on earth, Columbus' sailing west, etc. Initially old school texts from the public school system were used. In recent years teachers have developed their own texts in mathematics for all grades, geography for those in grades four to six, phonetics for grades one and two, as well as history texts for the students in grades seven and eight, *Pleasant Places* and *A Goodly Heritage*. The latter project required extensive research and writing, and are void of the focus upon war as seen in public school texts. These texts include some Mennonite history as well.

Each school has its own school board consisting of three men. Costs of the entire school system include the teachers' salary, custodial care, cost of books, and

administration. These monies are collected through the church deacons. The local school board is responsible for hiring, done in early March, as well as the upkeep of the building and school yard, and expansion, should this be necessary. The school system is the largest bureaucratic structure found among the OOMs, and it runs independent of the church structure. Parents of children in the school receive a tax deduction for their financial contribution, only after a base sum has been paid.

This school program differs vastly from the government's. Teachers usually live in the community and are known by the pupil's parents. Teaching does not include the use of videos or computers. Teachers have not taken university courses in child psychology. The individual's likes or aspirations are subservient to the group's needs. Students are not encouraged to pursue interests in science or literature. School has a very pragmatic goal; to prepare the child for adult life in the old order community. In school they have frequent contact with others outside their own grade. At times the older assist the younger. There is no fuss at graduation, with an anticipation to enter high school. There is no group culture with a fashion, sports, movie star or dress/hair style focus, and almost no student "school sucks" sentiment. The Christmas program is comprised of songs and poems, some pitted with humour. Parents and grandparents enjoy this occasion. The school year terminates with a picnic and sports activities.

X
Economics
Work For Living, Happiness, God and Others

The old order economic system functions in marked contrast with the capitalist system. Wealth for wealth's sake is despised. Conspicuous consumption is considered hideous. Some forms of technology, though more efficient, are shunned. Advertising is very minimal. Government lobbying is forbidden. Aid from government sources is generally not accepted.

Their economics is rural based. Both historically and in the present, agriculture is the preferred means of livelihood. Most are fully or partially dependent upon dairy, beef, and to a lesser degree hogs and poultry. All farming is done by older and smaller machinery compared to their non-Mennonite neighbours. Their acreage is between eighty and 170, their dairy herd no more than forty, in contrast to the six hundred acres and 150 milking cows of some farmers nearby. They experience the same fluctuations in price, climate, and interest rates as others. Trucks pick up milk from diary farms every second day, and those raising beef or hogs have scheduled weekly transport of their stock to the market.

For youth, work away from home begins at age fourteen or fifteen, when a relative or neighbouring farmer needs assistance for a few days. Young girls help with house duties, often in a family which has a newborn, and young lads assist with harvesting and building. More serious employment begins at about age sixteen. A girl's parents receive up to two hundred dollars monthly. If the father can handle farm duties along with younger teen-age sons, an older son "contracts" out to another farmer for a year. The monthly or annual cheque is paid to his father, which later aids the young man when he begins life on his own at marriage. Hired male help is about four to five hundred dollars monthly, but varies with experience, and includes room and board. At times an adjustment is made if he has his own buggy. In each case such assistants enter fully into the activity of their resident family. These farm experiences augment youths' understanding of their future vocations.

Employers, whether in a shop, farm, or kitchen are not to be severe or demand hard labour of their hired hands. They are to instruct the young person in running the household, farm, or shop. Often the location is distant from the family of the hired help, and he or she may not see his or her family for a month or two at a time. Agreements with hired help have their own norms and are not made in writing. Men make arrangements in June, and women in September, with service beginning in January, usually for a twelve month period. One's word is sufficient. If for some reason it is not upheld, which is rare, word will spread in the community. In the event that a crisis arises at the home farm where assistance is required, the hired hand is free to leave.

No old order could begin farming without the unusual consideration given him from the community. All parents make every effort, at financial cost, to have their son become established in a vocation at marriage. The community responds when parents cannot. Many begin at age twenty-four or twenty-five in a near-million-dollar farm operation, with loans from community as well as the Mennonite Savings and Credit Union or other banks. They work hard, and many, for the first few years, are under the guidance of parents or community members who have loaned them money.

Almost every young farmer has a keen savvy, and occasionally a bit of justified pride in his farming. He observes the weather, and chooses a time to seed and harvest accordingly. He knows when and how to process animal feed. He cares for his herd, and has a veterinarian attend when necessary. He knows breeding and calving. He keeps his machinery in repair and knows how to weld. He spends long hours, from dawn until after dark, to make the operation viable. Financing is a challenge, but he has endurance. His father and grandfather worked the land and survived. Hard labour is not to be avoided. He finds it rewarding to harvest a field of

hay, wheat, or full stocks of corn. He enjoys being outside in the elements, free from employer dependency.

Joint farm labour is often required throughout the year. This may occur for making silage, haying, threshing, firewood cutting, and corn harvesting. Men share their implements and tractors, and tally the time spent on the others' fields. At the end of their labours, they appropriately pay any imbalance.

If the farmer has idle time in the winter or for a few weeks in the summer, he may engage in other wage-earning activity. Many are fully engaged when the frost breaks in spring, collecting sap from maple trees for syrup. A few farmers have as many as two thousand trees, and are engaged for almost six weeks, preparing, processing, and then cleaning at the end of the season. Many have carpenter shops in which they show their skill by making kitchen cupboards, shelves, bed frames, chests of drawers, cedar chests, tables, and chairs. Others join a construction crew of fellow old orders and build sheds, smaller barns and homes for those in their community and outside it. Some older men find daily employment in a shop run by one of the David Martin group. Several do horseshoeing and related iron work. Other enterprises serve both the Mennonite and outside community: harness-makers, buggy-makers, wood-benders, foundries for stoves and the metal pieces for harnesses. Courier trucks stop by on a thrice-weekly basis. Single men are engaged in the same vocations as married men.

Other men have earnings from unique sources such as bookkeeping and filing taxes, teaching, tractor and farm machinery sales, saw-milling, selling seed and binder twine, organic farming with the use of appropriate equipment, or breeding dogs for Toronto pet stores. The ingenuity for work-at-home business is extensive. In general, there is greater community tolerance for an older person working outside the community. Whatever temptations exists from the outside, it is viewed as less threatening.

Women's employment is possibly more varied. About half do housekeeping, for parents, a brother, the elderly, and a few for households that are non-Mennonite. All female schoolteachers are single, and earn between six and ten thousand dollars for their ten months of service. Other employment includes baking, seamstressing (for both married and single women), quilting, operating a grocery, fabric or handicraft store, market gardening, day work in factories, cleaning, and babysitting. A few married women, mostly those over age forty-five, find their niche in an activity in the house, such as sewing, or in a store. Every capable adult is expected to work for his or her own upkeep. This proves to be challenging for many single women. In some cases sisters or friends purchase a house together. They are more likely to live in a village.

The following story will help us understand the old order way of doing business. Since the early seventies there has been a growing population in the Mount Forest area, some eighty kilometres to the north of the Waterloo and Peel regions. Relatives and friends wish to visit one another. They have hired a commercial bus to make specific stops at marked times on a designated route between the two points twice a week. Riders do not pay the driver, nor do they record their travel. An honour system is used, wherein travellers send money to a treasurer who keeps the books. The system was initiated March 7, 1988, works well, and has no functional link with the church. This shows trust, and a bare minimum of bureaucracy.

XI Government

An Unpleasant Institution ...
To Be Tolerated

Perspective

Old order people feel the government is ordained by God, and seek in every way to respect and obey it. In their Sunday service they pray for the government. It functions to maintain order and to punish those who do wrong. However, they believe God is the supreme authority. When belief conflicts with the law, they feel they must differ with the government, even at great cost and possible suffering.

From the writings of Paul, they feel they should, "Bear ... one another's burdens" (Galatians 6:2) and " ... provide ... for those in [their] own house ..." (1 Timothy 5:8). They feel it is the responsibility of the church community to care for those within its group. Any compromise would lead an individual or family to depend upon other sources, like the government. Such a practice would shift members' allegiance away from the church community and God.

Old orders make a clear distinction between church and state. Government is pressured by lobby groups, and politicians often seek either their own interests or the interests of special groups. To avoid being tainted by anything evil in politics, they do not seek office, nor do they vote. Their sense of right living, or Christian living, includes being peculiar. One is to " ... come out from among them, and be separate"(2 Corinthians 6:17), and " ... not belong to the world" (John 17:16). One is to " ... keep oneself untainted from the world" (James 1: 27). This would include any interface with government.

Practice

There are a number of ways OOMs could financially benefit from the government. They refuse all government assistance programs. By law, like all other citizens, OOMs

69

contribute to Canada Child Tax Benefits. They refuse this benefit. (This now amounts to $203.66 monthly for an eligible mother with one child. Currently, at age sixty-five, Canadian citizens receive $442.66 monthly through Old Age Security.) Those in need receive additional funds from the Guaranteed Income Supplement. OOMs refuse these monies. However, the David Martin group and the Markham group do receive these monies.

In 1966 the government introduced the Canada Pension Plan, whereby all employers and employees pay a percentage of their monthly wage to a fund. Its purpose is "to make financial provision for their retirement and to protect themselves and their dependents or survivors against loss of income in the event of disability or death." OOMs view this as an insurance policy, and prefer to be interdependent within the religious community, thus they felt they could not participate. Initially the government garnished monies from their bank accounts, and their milk and beef sales. A tentative agreement was made, and currently they are seeking a further resolution.

The sole purpose of the government's introduction of the Social Insurance Numbers (SIN) program was to keep close track of all recipients of Old Age Pension. The old orders resisted this move, considering it a serious compromise with the world. They felt it would eventually be used in matters beyond those of the social insurance program, despite assurances that it would not. Their hunch and sense proved correct. These numbers play a central role in our society, and are used extensively by the government, banks, and employment agencies. Most do not object to the use of numbers. OOMs are opposed to a numbering system designed for accessing the programs their conscience does not permit them to be involved in. They are now exempt from the SIN, and have another government number for their special category.

Canada requires that all employees and employers participate in Employment Insurance and Worker's Compensation. Small OOM businesses throughout the countryside hire from one to a dozen employees. For years they have accepted these labourers as co-owners, avoiding this "insurance." They are now seeking another acceptable alternative. Ontario law requires all farmers who earn over seven thousand dollars to register with either of the two unions, Ontario Federation of Agriculture or the Christian Farmers Federation of Ontario. In 1999 OOMs were exempt from joining these unions for religious reasons. Under this provision they receive farmer tax exemptions.

Since 1966 OOMs and the Markham group have operated their own schools. Children generally remain at home after the termination of the term in which they have their fourteenth birthday. A small minority take additional courses by correspondence. The goal is to better train youth for skills necessary to make a livelihood in their way of life. They are conscientious about this goal. By age twenty young women have learned to bake, cook, care for children, quilt, sew, and organize all the responsibilities of the household. Most young men learn all the intricate details of farming in terms of animal care, seeding and harvesting hectares of grain crops, machinery maintenance and building construction. Some learn the craft of harness-making, horseshoeing, carpentry or cabinet-making. The community wishes to continue this practice of skill training after their formal schooling. Currently the education system of OOMs, as well as that of other small private rural schools, is confronted with rigid government requirements regarding processed drinking water in schools.

Here are a number of other smaller matters that OOMs encounter with the government. By Ontario law, all organizations place a hundred-thousand-dollar bond with the government for each cemetery. Old orders feel this is an infringement upon their own corporate responsibilities. Joining the Amish, they persuaded the government that they would take this responsibility corporately. All gun owners must register, and must take a course in firearms. With the bishop's signature, they are exempt from the required photo on the license. Similarly, with a letter from the deacon, they are exempt from jury duty.

In an attempt to minimize pollution of soil and waters in rural areas, the government provides seventy-five per cent of the cost of pollution control projects. OOMs view this as a "handout." They do not accept the money, but do build manure storage sites, and some have hired environmentalists to address water run-off in a more nature-oriented way. OOMs have no difficulty in complying with new standards for lights and signage on horse or tractor-drawn vehicles. They rub shoulders with the law when the growth of marijuana plants is found in their corn fields. Such cultivation by outsiders is not unusual. In one case a farmer's son quickly reported by phone a perpetrator in the field, and authorities were able to arrest him in his car a few kilometres from the farm.

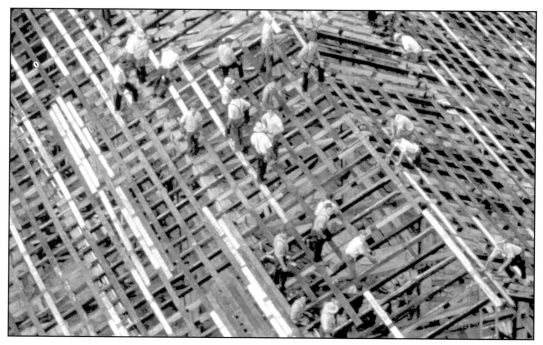

XII   Mutual Aid
The Community as Insurance

The unexpected happens. A mother of four young children is bedridden for four months, and dies. A father, now with a family of young teen-aged children loses his right hand in a feed grinder. Someone is sued for thousands of dollars because the signal for turning his horse and buggy was not recognized by the driver of the motor vehicle. An arsonist destroys farmer Martin's barn full of livestock. What financial and personal assistance is available among a people who find insurance policies, public health plans and social worker guidelines untenable?

OOMs have a proven response which predates any insurance plan, and which they claim is much more human. Should a building burn down, while the embers are still smouldering a committee of from three to five couples is planning and organizing. The farmer agrees to a building blueprint, and the committee hires a head carpenter, bulldozer and cementer. The necessary lumber and materials are purchased. Within days or weeks more than 250 willing hands will be on site to replace the structure. Women organize the feeding of the workers. This plain and simple response engages everyone in the community. Many apply their muscles to reconstruction. Some loan money for the project, and are paid back by the larger community once all expenses have been tallied. Up to twenty-five per cent of the actual expense is paid by the farmer himself.

A road accident involves an old order, and a claim is made by the motorized insured driver, who may or may not be at fault. Old orders are caught in a libel system in which they will not participate. They are not insured, oppose going to court, cannot make an oath in court because of conscience, do not condone the "wheeling and dealing of court," and refuse any negotiation to maximize one's financial gain. However they wish to be responsible. In such matters they seek a

73

reasonable settlement, and the entire community bears the cost, whether their member is guilty or not.

One is ill and cannot function to do farm work, or look after home and family duties. Adult siblings and aging parents immediately offer help, in both giving aid to the ill person, and doing required work. If required, several men in the community will do the harvesting. If at all possible, the sick person will be cared for at home, following specific instructions from the medical profession. In a few cases a professional visits weekly. When the family is unable to look after all required care, specific times are allotted so that others in the community will be present for twelve-hour shifts, to be with the ill or aged through the night or day.

The constituency addresses illness in a very personable way. Visits to shut-ins are frequent. (In one case parents had to urge visitors out of the house at 9:00 p.m. so that they might get adequate rest for the next day's work.) Groups numbering up to thirty youth, young couples, or senior members visit the shut-in to sing for almost two hours. Members in the community often produce a "sunshine" book, filled with pictures, prose or poems which are drawn, written, or cut out. Recipients take great delight in such thoughtfulness. Visitation to those in the hospital, regardless of the distance, is frequent.

Similarly, adults unable to live independently may reside with different families, two weeks at a time. Up to seventy-five per cent of all costs of medication and hospital are covered by the community. Two church collections for this cause are made annually. Deacons have the responsibility of handling these funds. There are a few cases where the elderly require continuous professional care. A couple of homes for seniors in nearby villages with old order staff provide this care. There are several physical and mentally challenged children who attend a local, publicly-funded daycare centre. OOMs as a church body financially support this institution. The community also has a "welfare" fund available to assist those with inadequate monies for livelihood.

Funds required by newlyweds to begin farming have been covered earlier. Similarly, community is evident in coaching new farmers. Farmers who face very adverse financial difficulties are also assisted. Schools are also funded by the entire membership, with monies channelled through the bookkeeping of a selected deacon.

Reflection

Now What do we Make of all This?

This is not a perfect world. There are inadequacies among the OOMs that outsiders readily identify. First, it appears that the group focus does not leave room for individual self esteem. This may be the cost of attention given to community. Or is the world outside the OOMs too focused on the individual? Our world often glorifies the individual to unnecessary heroic proportions at great cost to the common good. Second, are OOMs not bound by tradition to the detriment of the present? One can invert the question, and ask, "Do we give attention to the present to the point of ignoring the strength and good of the past?" Thirdly, the cost to someone within the community who does not fit is high. He or she must leave, and thereby lose the support and surroundings of their earlier social community and family. Some who leave find adjusting to the independence within the larger society difficult, at least initially.

OOM life does raise questions worth examining. This relates to our institutions of democracy, equality, financial aid, health care, family, education, and business practices. OOMs present an alternative. Their mode of life with a unique history, a fulcrum which is religious, in a rural setting, comprised of a few thousand people, would not suit a nation of over thirty million people who are mostly urban, living in a varied geography. However there are aspects of the OOM community worthy of our serious consideration.

Life can go on and have significant meaning without rampant advertising and consumerism. Businesses can become too big! The end of wealth and success is not more wealth and more success. There is a point where enough is enough! In the western social order people are hurt psychologically, physically, and materially. OOMs show us that much can be accomplished without a massive system of bureaucracy. Sometimes small is beautiful and the "simple" is satisfying. Civil activity on the local level has benefits that cannot be replaced by parliamentarians removed from their constituents. Volunteer work, already present to some degree in our society, is a very worthwhile activity.

Among the OOMs significant learning does take place outside the formal institution. Have we placed too much importance upon our conventional means of twelve years of required education? Often we augment secondary school with several more years of college or university. While it is stimulating and constructive for many, education may be over-rated. What viable options exist, and which are worth trying?

Are there not aspects of the past which are worth keeping and appreciating? Why is the new considered "exciting" and "awesome" simply because it is new and different? Do we not see that fashion comes at a high price, and has a very brief lifespan? Our wants go so far beyond our needs that millions in the South are deprived of the basics of survival. Many barely cope. We recognize that we produce mountains of waste which pollute our environment, but we fail to constrain this perennial lust.

While we might smart from the authority patterns within the OOM family, we see a monetary and care system which is extremely benevolent to each youth entering a vocation. We are impressed with the almost total absence of delinquency among youth. We note that even thirty-two-year-olds give heed to the voices of older people. Seniors have a wealth of experience, and might just have a word or two worth hearing. Our rhetoric of equality for all, from age eighteen to eighty-eight, may simply not give a society the most wholesome direction and wisdom.

OOMs tell us something about personal care for the sick. This care involves the touch of hands and the sight of faces from within the family and community. The community goes out of its way to make rehabilitation and companionship happen from within, rather than with strangers in a distant and foreign location (hospital), whenever possible. Through the OOM experience we learn that the non-professional can grasp and apply some methods of care within the home. Neighbourhood participation in many aspects of everyday life is a rich asset.

Many people struggle with the reality of earning a livelihood, and to some strongly-held ethical principles, in a larger and more pervasive economic structure which is inconsistent and imperfect. Old orders try to make it work, and adapt, even at great financial cost. Their principles of faith are the foundation of such living, which they do not verbally articulate. They wish to remain the quiet in the land, without doing harm to others. They would be grateful if we did the same toward them. Let's leave room to learn from one another.

APPENDIX

I. Dutch and Swiss Mennonite origins

Mennonite people have their roots in the Palatinate-Alsace (now France-Switzerland) of Europe and in the Netherlands. Many refer to the former as Swiss Mennonites and the latter as Dutch Mennonites (and sometimes, Russian). The Swiss movement broke from other Reformers, and soon thereafter the Dutch priest, Menno Simons, through his study of the Bible, felt compelled to join the movement in 1536. They were called Mennists or Mennonists, then later Mennonites. They found church practices of the day inconsistent with the sacred writings. They differed from other Reformers in at least three areas: 1. Baptism should take place when a person is capable of making a decision whether to accept the Christian life or not (as a youth or adult), not in infancy. 2. Religious matters should not be mixed with matters of the state. 3. People who follow Jesus' way should seek peace in all areas of life, even if it means hardship and misunderstanding. They also taught that Christians should avoid the courts and refuse to swear to any oath. (Doesn't a good person always tell the truth, and therefore not require an oath?)

As a result of their beliefs, they encountered severe persecution and many died at the stake.[1] Many of the Dutch emigrated to Poland soon after 1642. With an invitation from Katherine the Great, many migrated to the Ukraine beginning in 1780. As land became scarce, they expanded their migration to other parts of Russia. Ninety years later about 18,000 "Dutch" Mennonites emigrated to Canada and the

---

[1] See Thielman J. van Braght. *Martyrs Mirror: The Story of Seventeen Centuries of Christian Martyrdom From the Time of Christ to A.D. 1660.* 2nd ed. Trans. from the Dutch edition of 1660 by Joseph F. Sohm. (Scottdale: Herald Press, 2001).

United States. Twenty-one thousand more emigrated to Canada in 1922-1930, and 4,000 to South America. In 1943 about 35,000 Mennonites from Russia moved with the German army to Germany; however, 23,000 were forced to return. Of the remaining 12,000, some 7,000 eventually migrated to Canada and the others to Uruguay, Paraguay, and Brazil.

The Swiss Mennonites also suffered persecution. Their migration follows a different route. William Penn, a Quaker, invited them to Pennsylvania as early as 1710. Because of the American Revolutionary War, some migrated by horse and Conestoga wagon across the Niagara river, to Ontario, beginning in 1786. They farmed, built grain mills and sawmills, and some grew tobacco and worked distilleries. They lived like their contemporaries by farming and attending church on Sundays. We may wonder where the term "old" came from? In Canada in the 1880s a more pietistic mode of Christian life infiltrated this group of Mennonites. (Their United States counterparts addressed this situation about a decade earlier.) This new mode included Sunday School teaching for youth and children, a Sunday night service, and Wednesday prayer meetings. Some of the Swiss Mennonites had already joined other church groups. The more conservative group opposed this more modern trend, sensing this to be a movement away from tradition and the valued teaching of godliness within the family itself. They also opposed higher education. As these Christian teachings and aspects of modernity hit Mennonite communities, the more conservative group felt their lifestyle of being separate and peculiar was threatened.

In 1889 the two Canadian Swiss groups separated. The larger population broke from their conservative associates and formed the Old Mennonite church. Women in the newer "modern" group continued to wear coverings (small white "caps" on their heads) until about 1960. In 1988 they formed a union with a group of their Russian counterparts, the General Conference Mennonite Church, and identified themselves as the Mennonite Church of Eastern Canada. They now have ninety congregations and a baptized membership of over fourteen thousand. They belong to a national body, Mennonite Church Canada, with thirty-seven thousand baptized believers and over 250 churches. Until the eighties this Mennonite group in Ontario was readily identified ethnically by such names as Klassen, Thiessen and Friesen (Russian Mennonite) and Brubacher, Martin and Weber (Swiss Mennonite). Increasingly, anglophone names such as Smith, Hagan and Chard became part of the membership. In Quebec there are also francophone churches. Some Chinese,

Hmong, and Hispanic Mennonites have their own congregations, having become Mennonites in their respective countries before immigrating to Canada. Modern Mennonites enter fully into Canadian life. Some support their own schools of higher learning. Their foreign and local aid programs include the Mennonite Central Committee, Mennonite Economic Development Associates, and Mennonite Disaster Relief, which show their dedicated efforts to assist those in need. They also have work more directly through the church in programs among First Nations as well as people globally. Mennonites of Ontario have been categorized as either Conservative, Moderate or Progressive.[2] Moderates might number about twenty-two hundred baptized members, are almost all rural and use modern technology. They are distinct in that adult women wear head coverings, and men do not wear ties, but rather a Mao-type suit coat. They avoid movie theatres and dance halls, as well as the drinking of alcohol. They join modern Mennonites in the institution of banking, A few join larger groups for the festive singing of Christian anthems.

Suggested Readings:

see items in bibliography marked ★

II. The Amish

Many link Amish with old order Mennonites. Their leader, Jakob Ammann, wished to revitalize the church, and in 1693 broke from the Mennonite group. The crucial issue for him was a stricter observance of "shunning." This is the church's response of virtually no communication with those who are excommunicated. Amish now have a membership of over two hundred thousand, and have 250 settlements in the United States. Canada has seven settlements and a population of about fifteen hundred baptized members, all found in Ontario. They are located in the Aylmer (southeast of London) and Wellesley (west of Waterloo) areas. They differ from old order Mennonites in several ways. They do not have church buildings, but rather meet in houses or barns. Men grow a beard, but no moustache. They do not use tractors to farm, but rather horses. They do not use electricity. They have their own schooling program. Their bi-monthly publications are read in many old order

---

[2] See Fretz, J. Winfield. *The Waterloo Mennonites: A Community in Paradox.* (Waterloo, Ontario: Wilfrid Laurier University Press, 1989), 93.

Mennonite homes. Any unique issues they have with the government are likely similar to those found among the old order Mennonites.

There are numerous differences between Amish groups. Some drive black-covered buggies, others grey, yellow or white. Some allow telephones in their shops. Some permit milking machines, some mechanical balers. Gas-run refrigerators are allowed in some groups, and buttons on clothing in others.

Suggested Readings:

see items in bibliography marked◆

III. Summary of old order beliefs

Old orders are readily identified as those who use the horse and buggy for transportation, wear unique dress, and avoid the glitz of modern society. The seed of their being is much deeper. Kraybill and Bowman state their life philosophy as:

The individual is not the primary reality.
Communal goals transcend personal ones.
The past is as important as the future.
Tradition is valued over change.
Preservation overshadows progress.
New, bigger, and faster are not necessarily better.
Personal sacrifice is esteemed over pleasure.
Local involvement outweighs national acclaim.
Work is more satisfying than consumption.
Obedience to authority brings order and unity.
Spiritual salvation comes via the grace of community.
Friends are more important than status, fame, or wealth.
Yielding to community brings meaning, identity, and belonging.
Maintaining the unity of community is the supreme value.[3]

Suggested Readings on old order Mennonites.

see items in bibliography marked ⁂

---

[3] See Kraybill, Donald B. and Carl F. Bowman. *On the Backroad to Heaven*. (Baltimore: The Johns Hopkins University Press, 2001), 19.

Bibliography

Bible. New Revised Standard Version.

Burkholder, L. J. *A Brief History of the Mennonites in Ontario*. Kitchener: Mennonite Conference of Ontario, 1935.

★Dyck, Cornelius J. *An Introduction to Mennonite History*. Scottdale, Pa.: Herald Press, 1967.

★Epp, Frank H. *Mennonites in Canada, 1786-1920*. Toronto: MacMillan of Canada, 1974.

Epp, Marlene. *Mennonites in Ontario*. 2nd ed. Waterloo, Ontario: The Mennonite Historical Society of Ontario, 2002.

Fretz, J. Winfield. *The Waterloo Mennonites: A Community in Paradox*. Waterloo Ontario: Wilfrid Laurier University Press, 1989.

Frey, Levi and Edna. Interviews with author, Mount Forest, Ontario, 1996-2002.

✢Frey, Levi M. "Old Order Mennonite Mutual Aid Programs." *Ontario Mennonite History*. Vol. XX, No. 1 (May, 2002): 10-13.

✢Gingrich, Del. "The Plain and Simple Facts." St. Jacob's, Ontario: Visitor Centre brochure.

❖ Hiebert, Carl. *This Land I Love*. Waterloo County, Waterloo, ON: Gift of Wings Publishing, 2000.

❖ – – –. *Us Little People*. Toronto: Stoddart Publishing, 1998.

Horst, Isaac R. Interviews with author, Mount Forest, Ontario, 1994-2002.

❖ Horst, Isaac. *A Separate People: An Insider's View of Old Order Mennonite Customs and Traditions*. Waterloo, Ontario: Herald Press, 2000.

Interviews with numerous Old Order Mennonites who prefer not to be mentioned.

◆ Kraybill, Donald B. *The Riddle of the Amish Culture*. Baltimore: The Johns Hopkins University Press, 1989.

◆ Kraybill, Donald B. and Carl F. Bowman. *On the Backroad to Heaven*. Baltimore: The Johns Hopkins University Press, 2001.

Martin, Amsey. "Education Among the Plain People of Waterloo, Wellington and Perth Counties." *Ontario Mennonite History*. Vol. XX, No.1 (May, 2002): 9-10.

❖ Martin, Donald. *The Old Order Mennonites: Gelassenheit, Discipleship, Brotherhood*. Kitchener, Ontario: Pandora Press, 2003.

❖ Peters, John F. "The Old Order Mennonites: Application of Family Life Cycle Stages." C. Harvey, ed. *Maintaining our Differences: Minority Families Within Multicultural Societies*. London, England: Ashgate Publishers, 2001, 1-16.

❖ – – –. "The Old Orders as Canadian Citizens." *Ontario Mennonite History*. Vol. XX, No.1 (May, 2002): 2-9.

✢– – –. "Old Order Mennonite Economics." C. Redekop, V. Krahn & S. Steiner eds. *Anabaptist/Mennonite Faith and Economics*. Lanham, Maryland: University Press of America, 1993, pp. 153-176.

★Regehr T. D. *Mennonites in Canada 1939-1970*. Toronto: University of Toronto Press, 1996.

◆Steiner, Sam. "The crooked path: thirty years to integration in the Mennonite Conference of Eastern Canada." unpublished document, 2002.

Thieleman J. van Braght. *Martyrs Mirror: The Story of Seventeen Centuries of Christian Martyrdom From the Time of Christ to A.D. 1660*. 2nd ed. Trans. from the Dutch edition of 1660 by Joseph F. Sohm. Scottdale: Herald Press, 2001.

About Pandora Press

Pandora Press is a small, independently owned press dedicated to making available modestly priced books that deal with Anabaptist, Mennonite, and Believers Church topics, both historical and theological. We welcome comments from our readers.

Visit our full-service online Bookstore:
www.pandorapress.com

Pandora Press
33 Kent Avenue
Kitchener, Ontario
Canada N2G 3R2
Tel./Fax: (519) 578-2381
E-mail:
info@pandorapress.com
Web site:
www.pandorapress.com

Herald Press
616 Walnut Avenue
Scottdale, PA
U.S.A. 15683
Orders: (800) 245-7894
E-mail:
hp@mph.org
Web site:
www.mph.org